AF235636

WHO ARE YOU CALLING OLD?

SARAH CURTIUS

Bibliografische Information der Deutschen
Nationalbibliothek:

Die Deutsche Nationalbibliothek verzeichnet diese Publikation in der
Deutschen Nationalbibliografie; detaillierte bibliografische Daten
sind im Internet über http://dnb.dnb.de abrufbar.

Herstellung und Verlag: BoD – Books on Demand,
Norderstedt

ISBN: 978-3-7543-3070-8

Anyone who stops learning is old, whether at twenty or eighty. Anyone who keeps learning stays young.

Henry Ford

CONTENTS

ANTI-AGEING?

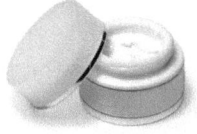

Vocabulary

From all walks of life is an idiom to talk about people with various different jobs and levels of education. It's used to talk about people representing all of society.

I learned a lot from my German teacher at school. German, obviously! But life wisdom, too. Mr Rich was in his sixties when he taught us and had a life full of stories to tell. I remember one lesson especially. We were in our mid-teens and were talking about how awful it must be to grow old. He smiled at us and said, "It's better than the alternative!"

He was right, of course. In the 60s, Roger Daltry and his band *The Who* sang "I hope I die before I get old!". Roger is now in his late seventies and I think he is glad he did not die before he got old!

People have always wanted to stop the ageing process. The ancient Romans and Greeks were the first to believe in a philosopher's stone which could turn other metals to gold and the "fountain of youth". In the Middle Ages, people called alchemists were still looking for the philosopher's stone and its special powers. Today, some people think they can find the same kind of magic in cosmetic surgery or Botox to get rid of wrinkles. Most of us hope we can find it in the anti-ageing creams we buy in the drugstore.

Why do we want to look younger? Advertising tells us that young is beautiful. We think that getting old means we cannot do certain things anymore and cannot learn new things. While being young is beautiful and healthy and exciting, being old means we become weak and ill and boring.

In this book I want to challenge the idea that ageing is all bad! We will learn about so many people who are still doing amazing and interesting things in 'old age'. We will look at people **from all walks of life** – famous people like singers, actors, a king and a queen, but also 'normal' people. Some of the people you will meet have always been active and successful in their area. Some only started something new late in life. What they all have in common is that they lived interesting lives and do not believe that getting old means becoming weak and ill and boring!

We will learn about what happens in our brains as we get older and get some tips to keep our brains healthy. We do not want to be 'anti-ageing'! We want to be pro-ageing! We all want to live a long and interesting life. If we do, it means we have to get old. Getting older means having a life of experience. Getting old does not have to be boring.

A group of 40 pensioners proved this in 2007. They recorded a version of *The Who*'s song, *Talking about my generation* in Abbey Road Studios. After appearing on the BBC, the group were asked to give interviews all over the world and even travelled to America. The lead singer, 90-year-old Alf summed it up by saying, "It's just brought me back to life. I was 90 and stuck in a rut. And now I feel that I have come alive again."

THE POWER OF MUSIC

We are never too old to make or enjoy music. When asked why he still practiced his cello at the age of 90, Pablo Casals answered, "Because I think I'm making progress." At the age of 100, the pianist Irving Fields advised, "Enjoy music to stay young at heart."

We are going to meet three musicians over 80 who still love music and who can say that it has helped them to stay young at heart: the two famous singers Sir Tom Jones and Tony Bennett, and music teacher Paul Harvey. All of them still make music and find great joy and fulfillment in it.

Tom Jones –
It's not unusual

Vocabulary

Coal is *black and hard and dug out underground in mines. The people who do this dangerous job are called* **miners**.

Tuberculosis is *a very serious disease which affects a person's lungs.*

The monarch in the UK can give honours to people who have done something special. There are lots of different awards but some of the most common are a **knighthood**, a CBE (Commander of the British Empire), an OBE (Order of the British Empire) and an MBE (Member of the British Empire). Someone who is made a **knight** or a **dame** (for a woman) are called **Sir** or **Dame**. A number of people in this collection have been given one of these special honours.

Tom Jones was born in 1940 in Pontypridd, a small town in a valley of South Wales. His father worked as a **miner** in the **coal** mines. Tom did not enjoy school and was very ill with **tuberculosis** as a child. There was one thing that Tom did love – singing.

He sang with various bands and was spotted by a music manager who took him to London. In 1965, Tom had his first hit: *It's not unusual*. He had a number of big hits in the UK and the US, including *The green, green grass of home* and *Delilah*. He sang the title song for the James Bond movie *Thunderball* in 1965.

Tom has always loved to work with other singers and became a close friend of Elvis Presley. He had his own TV show in America where he sang with lots of other stars. He has sung with many great singers, including Janis Joplin, Robbie Williams, Aretha Franklin and Johnny Cash. He appeared in some films and TV programmes.

In 2000, Bill Clinton asked Tom to sing at the New Year's celebrations in Washington DC. In 2006, Tom was made **Sir** Tom Jones by Queen Elizabeth II. In 2021, aged 80, Tom Jones released his 41st album called *Surrounded by Time*. This makes him the oldest artist to have a number 1 album in the UK. At 80, Tom Jones still has a wonderful baritone voice. Critics praised the album and some wrote that it was his most emotional album.

How does Sir Tom still sound so good at the age of 80? He says he is lucky and he is very grateful. He says he does not drink much alcohol anymore and he tries to stay fit. He is not giving up singing or slowing down. He says he will keep singing "as long as there's breath in my body".

Tony Bennett – Still singing at 94!

Vocabulary

If someone is **demoted***, then they are given a less important position or job.*

Anthony Dominick Benedetto was born to Italian-American parents in New York in 1926. The family was poor and Tony's father died when he was just 10 years old. However, his father had given his son a passion for music, literature and art and these passions have stayed with Tony all his life.

Tony started singing for money at 13 and becoming a professional singer was always his dream. Tony fought in the Second World War and stayed in Germany as part of the occupying American forces. He sang for the American forces while he was with the army in Germany. One day, he went out to eat with a black friend he knew from school. Black and white soldiers were not allowed to eat together in the US Army at that time and Tony was **demoted**. Tony always supported the Civil Rights Movement and in 1965, he took part in the marches from Selma to Montgomery with Martin Luther King.

He went back to America in 1946 and learned a special singing technique, *bel canto*. This helped him keep his voice in good condition throughout his life. In 1949, he was discovered by Bob Hope who took him on tour with him and gave him the name Tony Bennett.

Tony was very successful in the 1950s and 60s but when *The Beatles* new style of pop music arrived in the 60s, Tony's style of jazz and swing music went out of fashion. Tony went through a very difficult phase and developed a drug addiction which nearly killed him.

His son Danny believed that young people would like Tony's style of music if they had the chance to hear it again. Danny became Tony's manager and he arranged for his father to play on the new music television channel MTV. Danny was right. Young people loved his father's music.

Tony continued making music and sang with lots of other famous singers. At the age of 88, he recorded an album with Lady Gaga. This made him the oldest person ever to have a number 1 album in the US.

Tony Bennett also paints and signs his artworks with his birth name, Benedetto.

Tony Bennett has continued to perform and make records. He has sold over 50 million records and won many awards, including 20 Grammys. He supports charities with both his time and his money.

In 2021, it was revealed that Tony had been diagnosed with Alzheimer's disease in 2016. Despite the diagnosis, Tony kept singing, giving concerts and recording until the Covid pandemic hit in 2020. A second album with Lady Gaga is set to be released in 2021. His doctor believes that his regular singing practice stopped Tony from suffering worse symptoms of the disease.

In an interview in 1999, Tony pointed to artists like Picasso who had kept painting until they died and said, "If you are creative, you get busier as you get older." This seems to have been his motto and it appears to have done him good.

Paul Harvey –
An inspirational music teacher

Vocabulary

A **party trick** *is something special or surprising that people perform at parties to surprise friends and family.*

If something **goes viral** *it means that it is very popular and spreads very quickly on the internet.*

Paul Harvey was an inspirational music teacher at a local school in the south of England. A number of his students became professional musicians. Paul also loved to compose music. As a **party trick**, a friend or family member would give him four notes and immediately he would compose a piece of music with those notes on the piano. This is an amazing talent and when Paul's son filmed his father doing this in August 2020, the video went **viral**. What made this even more amazing is that 80-year-old Paul suffers from dementia.

His son says that if Paul is having a bad day, playing the piano really helps him. The piece of music Paul composed was so beautiful that the BBC Philharmonic Orchestra recorded it and it went to number one.

Scientists have found that the parts of the brain which remember songs are generally not affected by dementia. They also found that old songs are closely linked to things that happen in our lives. We remember music we listened to when we were between 10 and 30 especially well. Playing music from this period can really help people who are beginning to suffer from dementia. More and more groups are encouraging people with dementia and their carers to join choirs. The effects are very positive.

Music is good for us. Just listening to music improves how our brain works. It has a positive effect on language. It makes us feel good because it lowers the stress hormone cortisol. Listening to our favourite music can even make pain less painful! Maybe it is time to put some music on and dance around the kitchen!

THE BRAIN

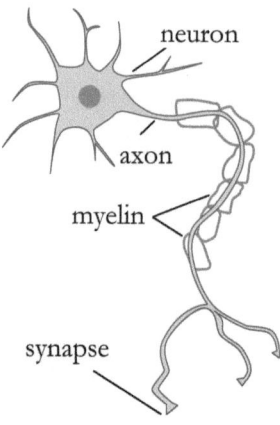

We all have a brain ... but do you know how your brain works and what it looks like inside? The brain is a fascinating organ. We are going to learn a little bit about how amazing it is. Of course, not everyone believed it was important. The ancient Egyptians knew how important other organs were, like the heart and the stomach but when they mummified their rulers, they pulled the brain out through the nose and threw it away! In fact, we did not know very much about the brain until very recently. Most of what we know has been discovered since the beginning of the 21st century.

Your brain weighs 1.5 kg. Although the brain is not that large, it uses 20% of the body's energy. In general, a man's brain is 10% bigger than a woman's brain. But with brains, size does not matter! Einstein's brain was also smaller than average.

The brain is made up of 86 billion brain cells or **neurons**. When people talk about 'grey matter' or 'little grey cells' they are talking about the neurons. Each neuron makes connections to other neurons. These connections are called **synapses**. Each neuron can have 7,000 to 10,000 connections to other neurons. Between birth and their 2nd birthday, a baby develops 1.8 million synapses ... every second! As adults we have between 100 and 150 **trillion** synapses! 100 trillion is 100,000,000,000,000.

The part of the neuron which forms the connection to another neuron is called the **axon**. The axon is covered with a fatty substance called **myelin**. This myelin is white. That is where the term 'white matter' comes from. Myelin is produced throughout childhood until we are about 20 years old. Without the myelin, impulses in the brain can travel 10 metres per second. With the myelin, they travel 100 metres per second!

When we learn something, we form new connections between the neurons. Learning changes what our brain looks like. Your brain is as unique as your fingerprints.

One more amazing but strange fact: Did you know you actually have two 'brains'? Your intestines also have neurons which produce important chemicals.

By ROYAL APPOINTMENT

The present Queen of the United Kingdom and Northern Ireland, Elizabeth II, celebrated her 95th birthday in 2021. No-one has ruled for as long as she has and she is still mentally and physically active.

In this chapter, we are going to learn a little about one king of Great Britain from the 19th century and a queen of England from the Middle Ages. King William IV was the oldest person to become king when his brother died without a surviving child. Queen Eleanor was one of the most powerful women of the Middle Ages. She was the ruler of Aquitaine, Queen of France and later, Queen of England.

King William IV
(1765-1837)

Vocabulary

A **Regent** is someone who rules because the king or queen is ill or too young.

Gout is a painful disease that makes your joints swell and hurt.

William IV was 64 when he became King of Great Britain and Ireland and King of Hanover in June 1830. He was the third son of King George III who ruled for nearly 60 years. George and his wife, Queen Charlotte had 15 children. The family lived in the Palace in Kew Gardens. George was a very religious man, who prayed for hours every day. He lived a simple life and the newspapers called him 'Farmer George'.

George III went mad and was not able to rule for the final ten years of his reign. His eldest son, George became **Prince Regent** and ruled for his father. The Prince Regent finally became King George IV when his father died but only ruled for ten years and died at the age of 67. George's next living brother became king after him. This was William IV.

William had joined the Navy when he was just 13. He fought in several battles and in the American War of Independence. While William was in America, George Washington planned to kidnap him but the British heard about the plan and guards protected him. William became good friends with Horatio Nelson.

From 1791, William lived with an Irish actress who called herself Mrs Jordan. They were very happy together for 20 years and had five sons and five daughters.

As William's elder brothers had no children, William knew that at least one of them should have a child who could become king or queen in the next generation! So, William left Mrs Jordan and married the German princess Adelaide of Saxe-Meiningen in 1818. The marriage was happy but sadly, all of their children died young.

George IV loved luxury. The newspapers of the time wrote about him spending money on expensive building projects, art, fashion, parties and women. He ate and drank too much and suffered from **gout**. William was very different. He gave up alcohol when he got married and lived a simple life. He walked for hours every day, often wandering around London without guards. He was popular with the people.

George III had bought Buckingham House and George IV had then spent a lot of money rebuilding it to look like the palace it is today. However, William hated and tried to give it to Parliament when the old Houses of Parliament burned down in 1834. Unfortunately for William, the Members of Parliament did not like it either! Instead, they built the building on the bank of the Thames which you can still see today.

William and Adelaide loved their niece, Princess Victoria, but did not get on well with her mother. William died in June 1837, just a month after Victoria turned 18. This meant that Victoria could become queen and her mother, the Duchess of Kent, would not be Regent.

Hanover had become a kingdom in 1814, at the Congress of Vienna after the wars with Napoleon, so George III, George IV and William IV were all kings of Hanover as well as Great Britain and Ireland. However, Victoria could not become queen of Hanover if there was a living male relative. With this, the so-called "personal union" between the kingdoms came to an end. Victoria became Queen of Great Britain and Ireland and William's younger brother Ernest Augustus became King of Hanover.

Although none of King William and Queen Adelaide's children survived, his children with Mrs

Jordan did, and one famous descendant is the former British Prime Minister David Cameron.

William was the oldest person to become the British monarch. If Prince Charles lives longer than his mother Queen Elizabeth II, he will become the oldest person to become monarch. At the time of writing, Charles is already 72 years old.

Queen Eleanor of Aquitaine (1122-1204)

———

Vocabulary

The **Crusades** were wars between Christians and Muslims which started in the 11th century.

If a marriage is **annulled**, it means that the couple was never really married. The reason was often that the marriage had not been consummated, but it could also be because the couple decided they were too closely related.

A **nun** is a woman who has promised to serve God and not marry. She often lives in a **convent** with other nuns, called sisters. Men who live like this are called monks and live in a monastery.

———

Eleanor was born in 1122 in Poitiers in France and grew up to become the most powerful woman of the Middle Ages. Her father was William X, Duke of Aquitaine, the largest and richest province in France. He made sure that Eleanor was well educated. She learned Latin, arithmetic and history as well as dancing, playing the harp, singing, riding and sewing. Eleanor was intelligent and strong-willed.

In 1130, her mother and younger brother died. Seven years later, Eleanor's father also died, and Eleanor became the ruler of Aquitaine.

The King of France, Louis VI (also called Louis the Fat) was responsible for Eleanor now. Eleanor was the richest woman in France and so Louis married her to his son, also called Louis. Louis VI died just a few weeks after the wedding, and Eleanor and her husband became King and Queen of France. Eleanor was beautiful and lively and Louis was in love with her. Their daughter Marie was born in 1145.

Eleanor and Louis went on the **Second Crusade to the Holy Land** but it went badly. Their marriage began to suffer. They had another daughter but Eleanor did not want to stay married to Louis. In 1152 their marriage was **annulled** because she said he was a close relative. Eight weeks later Eleanor married Henry, Duke of Normandy, even though he was an even closer relative!

Two years later Henry became Henry II, King of England. The marriage to Henry was at least as difficult as the marriage to Louis but Eleanor had eight children with him, while Henry also had children with other women. In 1167, Eleanor left Henry and England and returned to Aquitaine. She lived there for six years until her sons rebelled against their father. Eleanor probably helped them, and Henry arrested her and took her back to England. She was a prisoner in England for 16 years.

When Henry died in 1189, their son Richard the Lionheart became King. While Richard was away on the **Third Crusade**, Eleanor took an active role in ruling the country. Richard died and his brother John became King. Eleanor outlived all of her children except John and one of her daughters. She was active throughout her whole life. At the age of 77, she set off to choose one of her granddaughters as the bride for the French king, Philip II.

She never went back to England. She became a **nun** at the **convent** in Fontevraud in France. She died aged 82. She is buried there next to her husband Henry, and their son Richard. She was a remarkable woman.

The older brain

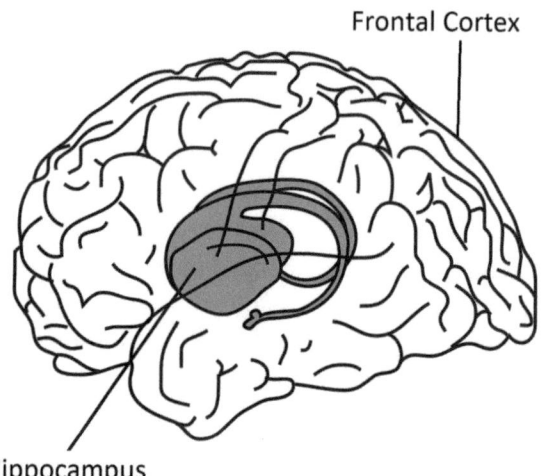

Frontal Cortex

Hippocampus

The brain develops until we are about 20. Between the ages of 20 and 50, there is little change. After that, the brain can start to change but everyone experiences these changes and the speed of change differently. Generally, two important areas can start to shrink. These are the **frontal cortex** and the **hippocampus**. They shrink because neurons die.

The frontal cortex is the part of the brain that plans, organises and checks our behaviour. The hippocampus is important for our long-term memory and for learning. Scientists think that the shrinking in these two areas is the reason we get more forgetful as we get older.

Myelin also decreases as we age. Scientists think this is why we are not so fast at working things out as we get older.

But it is not all bad news! For a long time, scientists thought that our brains shrink because no new neurons replace the ones that die. We now know that this is not true! Neurons are created throughout our lifetimes and we can still create connections (synapses) between these neurons. And there is even more good news! Most of the neurons are produced in the hippocampus, the area which is so important for memory and new learning. Thousands of neurons are created every day in the hippocampus. Sadly, they die after a few weeks unless they are used. If you learn something new, you give these neurons a good chance to survive. To put it another way: Use it or lose it!

How can we keep our brains healthy? There is an English proverb which says, "**A rolling stone gathers no moss**". In other words: Keep active! In this book, we will see lots of examples of people who kept their brains healthy. What they all have in common is that they are active. There are three main areas where it is good to keep active.

Keep physically active!

Physical activity increases blood to the brain and helps the body create new neurons. A good healthy diet is also important.

Keep mentally active!

It's important to keep busy and have interesting hobbies. Your hobby may be playing or learning a musical instrument, learning a language, or doing something creative like painting or doing a craft. These are all excellent things to keep your brain healthy. Reading is also good, especially reading books rather than short articles in magazines and newspapers. A good long story means that our brains have to concentrate for longer.

Keep socially active!

Spending time with other people is also really important to keep your brain healthy. Scientists found that loneliness made people more likely to develop high blood pressure and heart disease but also depression and cognitive decline. It is good to keep in touch with family and friends but you could also join a group and learn a new hobby.

ACTS OF KINDNESS

In 2020, the world was shaken by the Coronavirus pandemic. The news from many parts of the world was upsetting. In this period, many people did whatever they could to help friends, family and neighbours. People organised food, phoned and checked on people who could not leave their homes. Some sewed face masks and even **scrubs**, the special clothes which doctors and nurses could wear when they were working in the hospital. Some people did amazing things to raise money and, in this chapter, we look at four such people. Two of these people are 100 years old and two are under ten, but all of them raised money for others and made us smile and inspired us through a difficult time.

Captain Sir Tom Moore – Tomorrow will be a good day!

Thomas Moore was born and grew up in Yorkshire, England. When he was 20, he joined the British army. He trained as an officer and during the Second World War, he served in India and Western Burma (now Myanmar).

He left the army in 1946 but organised a reunion for his battalion every year for 64 years. He worked at different companies in the building trade when he left the army. In his free time, he loved to race motorbikes and won several races.

Tom led a quiet life with his wife and looked after her when she became ill. As he got older, he himself had a number of health problems and he moved in with his daughter and her family. In 2018, he fell. He broke his hip and had other injuries. He was treated in hospital and the medical staff loved him because he was always cheerful and kind. When he went for check-ups, he took chocolate for the doctors and nurses. In April 2020, in order to improve his strength after time in hospital, he started to walk around his daughter's garden. He wanted to raise £1,000 for the NHS who had looked after him so well. He called it "Tom's 100th Birthday Walk for the NHS".

By 10 April, the media had heard about Tom's walk. His story went around the whole world. On his

100th birthday on 30 April 2020, two historic World War II planes flew over Tom's house. Famous people wished him a happy birthday, including British Prime Minister Boris Johnson, Prince Charles and the Secretary-General of the United Nations, Antonio Guterres. By the evening of his birthday, he had raised nearly £33 million.

The Queen knighted Captain Tom Moore at Windsor Castle on a beautiful sunny day on 17 July 2020. In January 2021, he became ill and later tested positive for Coronavirus. He died on 2 February 2021. In 2020, a difficult year around the world, this quiet man became a symbol of hope. His walk gave many other people the inspiration and courage to do amazing things, too. The world will remember Sir Tom Moore as a brave, kind man who shared love and happiness and showed us how important it is to look after one another.

Tony and Frank –
Two little boys follow Sir Tom's example

Vocabulary

Spina bifida is a medical condition where the spine was not properly developed before the baby was born.

When people lose a limb (arm or leg), they sometimes receive an artificial arm or leg. We call this artificial limb a **prosthetic limb**.

Frank is six years old and has **spina bifida**. He lives in Bristol with his family and only learned to walk when he was 4. Frank saw Captain Tom Moore on TV and decided to try and raise £99 for the NHS by walking 10 metres with his walking frame every day.

Frank raised £280,000 and received a letter from Boris Johnson. "You are brave and brilliant just like [Captain Tom]," he wrote.

Another little boy who was inspired by Captain Tom was five-year-old Tony Hudgell. Tony was badly hurt by his parents when he was just a baby and nearly died. He lost both his legs and he is deaf in one ear. He was adopted and he is now a happy little boy. He walked 10 kilometres on his **prosthetic legs** and raised £1.3 million for the hospital where he is treated regularly.

Dabirul Islam Choudhury – Walking during Ramadan

Captain Tom inspired so many people to walk, run or climb to raise money for people affected by the pandemic. Dabirul Islam Choudhury lives in East London and during Ramadan in April and May 2020, he wanted to raise £1,000 for people who needed help in the UK and Bangladesh. Like Captain Tom, Dabirul was walking in his garden. He met his target of £1,000 within hours and in the end, he raised more than £420,000.

Daburil was born in British Assam (now Bangladesh) in 1920 and moved to the UK to study English literature in 1957. He is a well-respected leader in his community and a talented poet. He was given an OBE by the Queen. This award is given to people for service to the arts, science, or work for charities.

Give up your prejudices!

Vocabulary

A **prejudice** is a negative feeling or belief about a person or group of people which is not based on facts.

A **self-fulfilling prophecy** is when something bad happens just because you believe it will. For example, when traders on Wall Street get nervous and worried that prices will go down, they stop trading and so prices do go down.

When you think of **prejudices**, maybe you think of racism or sexism. It is sad but people are still treated differently or badly because of their skin colour or their sex. But what about ageism? Are people treated badly because of their age? Have you heard of ageism? Perhaps you have heard that young people or people over 50 can find it harder to find a job. Ageism affects children and young people, for example, when their needs are not taken seriously. However, ageism usually discriminates against older people.

But can older people be ageist? That sounds crazy, but sometimes older people can be prejudiced against themselves. No-one changes their skin colour but, if they are lucky, everyone grows old. Ageism is the only prejudice we can have against our own future selves.

Research shows that children begin to think of older people as weak or ill even before they start school. As we grow up, we never question these prejudices. We believe them throughout our lives and when we ourselves are older, they shape the way we see the world. What can these beliefs look like?

Perhaps we think we are too old to wear certain clothes or to do certain hobbies and this stops us from trying things out. Maybe we think we are too old to learn new things or learn to use new technology. Perhaps we believe that we will get more forgetful as we get older and there is nothing we can do about it. Or maybe we try to avoid looking our age, because we are afraid people will treat us badly if we look old.

Lots of studies have shown that having a negative view of ageing is very bad for you. In the Republic of Ireland, scientists are doing a study of 8,000 older adults (The Irish Longitudinal Study on Ageing TILDA). At the beginning of the study, the researchers recorded

- how fast people walked, a sign of how healthy someone is,
- how good their memory was,
- how much time they spent with other people, and
- what they thought of getting older.

Two years later, they found that those who had a negative view of ageing also walked slower, were mentally slower and had less social contact. It seems that if you believe that getting older is negative then it will be. It is a **self-fulfilling prophecy**.

As we have seen, the brain does not decline as much as people believe. Maybe we need a little longer to learn new things and a little more time to practice things so that they stay in our memories but we can still learn. Learning something challenging is good for the brain. It keeps us fresh!

What we believe is important. A negative view of ageing can damage our health and it can stop us from finding a new hobby or learning something new. A positive attitude to ageing, on the other hand, has a positive effect on our health and emotional wellbeing.

Born to run

"No sports! Just whisky and cigars!" This is what Winston Churchill is supposed to have said to a reporter. Churchill lived till he was 90 and lots of people would like to believe that smoking cigars, drinking whisky and doing no sports can help you live a long life. Churchill probably did not say that and it certainly is not very healthy! In this chapter we meet two women who show that the opposite is true. Julia Hawkins and Sister Madonna are exceptional athletes with wonderfully positive attitudes to life.

Julia 'Hurricane' Hawkins – World Record Holder

Julia Hawkins was born in Louisiana in 1916.

She has lived through both World Wars, the Great Depression, the Spanish flu pandemic and now the

Coronavirus pandemic. Julia "Hurricane" Hawkins is a World Record Holder: in 2019 she became the oldest woman to compete in a sporting competition in the United States. At the age of 103, Julia won both the 50- and 100-metre races. The surprising thing is that she did not take up running until she was 100!

Julia grew up in Louisiana. She met her husband at a party and the pair had to get married over the phone in 1942 because he was a soldier in the Second World War. Julia bought herself a bicycle as a wedding present. She was a teacher at a primary school which was seven miles away. There was a rubber shortage because of the war but Julia was one of the few people who were allowed to buy a bike because she needed it to get to work.

After the war, Julia and her husband settled in Baton Rouge and bought a house with an **acre** of land (a little more than 4000m^2). They were happily married for 70 years and raised their four children there. Julia was always active, loved gardening and always cycled to get the things she needed. At 75, she decided to enter the cycling event at the National Senior Games, an Olympic-style event for competitors over 50-year-olds.

At the games, she won bronze first and later gold. When she was 99, she had an accident with her bike and hurt her elbow. She decided it was time to give up cycling and she started running.

She does not run every day but she does bend and stretch. She says it is important to eat well, get enough sleep and keep busy. She grows bonsai trees in her garden and waters them every day. She loves flowers and often wears a flower in her hair, even when she runs at the games! Her eyesight is not as good as it was, so she cannot read very well any more. She listens to audiobooks now instead. She meets friends often and goes out for lunch with them. She is grateful for a happy life and loves spending time with her children, three grandchildren and two great-grandchildren.

Her most important advice is to keep physically and mentally active and to look for "magic moments": beautiful sunsets, beautiful birds or good things that happen to you. That is good advice!

Sister Madonna Buder – The 'Iron Nun'

Vocabulary

To find your calling *means that you have a strong feeling that you should do a certain job or activity.*

A **triathlon** is a race where athletes swim, then cycle and then run. The **Ironman** is a form of triathlon where the athletes swim 3.9 km, then cycle 180.2 km and finally run a marathon (42.2 km).

Gout is a painful disease that makes your joints swell and hurt.

———

Born in 1930 in St Louis, Missouri, USA, Marie Dorothy Buder decided that she wanted to become a nun, when she was 14. She served in a number of different convents until she found her second **calling**: running. She had never thought about running before. She was at a Christian conference in the late 1970s and a priest talked about how good running was for body, mind and soul. That night she left the hotel room and went for her first run.

She fell in love with running and joined a running group. That is where she first heard about the **Ironman** competition. She did her first **triathlon** in Ireland when she was 52. She swam without a wetsuit (they had not been invented yet) and cycled on a men's bike which she had bought at a police auction. Since then, she has done 400 triathlons, including 45 Ironmans. In 2005, when Sister Madonna was 75 years old, she did the Ironman in Hawaii. She was the oldest person ever to complete it.

In 1996, she completed an Ironman in 14 hours 27 minutes and 14 seconds – the World Record for people between 65 and 69 years old. She ran her final Ironman in Canada in 2012 when she was 82, when they had to create a new category for her: 80+.

She does not do Ironmans anymore but her last triathlon was in September 2019.

How does Sister Madonna train? She runs to church every day and cycles 64 km to go swimming in a lake. She also jogs to the prison where she visits the prisoners and reads the bible with them. Sister Madonna has written a book about her life called *The Grace to Race*.

What would Sister Madonna say to her younger self? "It's not what you say, it's what you do; don't pay attention to how old you are, only focus on how old you feel."

HEALTHY BODY, HEALTHY MIND

Vocabulary

A **toxic substance** is something which is very harmful for humans, animals or the environment. Toxic substances in your own body are often waste products made by the body.

mens sana in corpore sano –
A healthy mind in a healthy body
(Juvenal, 1st century AD)

In chapter 4 we saw how important it is to keep active – physically, mentally and socially. Both Julia Hawkins and Sister Madonna Buder are both physically very fit. Sister Madonna did her last triathlon at 89. Julia Hawkins took up running at 100. However, they have also kept active in the other two areas. Julia used to read books, but since her eyesight is failing she listens to audiobooks; Sister Madonna reads the Bible alone and with others. This keeps them mentally active. They both also have a lot of social contact with friends and family and in their communities. This keeps them socially active.

Maybe you have always loved doing sport and will carry on doing it as you get older. Maybe you have never done much sport. I think most people will not take up triathlon when they retire if they have never done any sport before. But is it still worth taking up sport as we get older?

Scientists agree that it is better if a person has always been physically active. Everyone knows that you are healthier if you have never smoked. However, we also know that, even if you have smoked all your life, your health will improve when you give it up, whatever your age. In the same way, scientists say that taking up some exercise at any time in your life will improve both your physical and brain health.

Exercise is obviously good for the body, but what happens to the brain when we exercise? Research has shown that 'moderate-intensity' exercise has a positive effect on the brain. Firstly, when we exercise, more blood gets pumped to the brain. Scientists believe that this helps prevent **toxic substances** building up. It also helps the brain create new neurons especially in the frontal cortex and the hippocampus. This is important as these are the two areas which can decline as we get older. What is 'moderate-intensity' exercise? This could be walking, swimming or cycling for 30 minutes at least three times a week.

Some people cannot exercise for health reasons. For them, scientists recommend doing lighter exercise like Tai Chi. Even small amounts of activity can be good for us.

Some research suggests that even standing is better for you than sitting! The University of Chester did a study with a group of people who normally sit all day at work. They asked them to stand for three hours instead. They noticed a number of health benefits on the days when people stood. Firstly, it helped their blood sugar levels go down after eating. We need blood sugar, but if the levels are too high, we can develop diabetes or heart disease.

They also found that standing makes our hearts beat faster than sitting. This means that we burn more calories. In fact, the scientists found that people burned up to 50 calories an hour more by standing than sitting. If you add this up for a whole year, then standing for three hours a day uses as many calories as running 10 marathons!

Perhaps you will not take up running when you are a hundred, but even a little exercise is better than none and can help you keep your brain healthy.

WRITE FROM THE HEART

Reading novels is certainly good for the brain but neuroscientist Jenni Ogden believes that creative writing is also good for the ageing brain. There is no reason why someone cannot write excellent stories as they get older. Our language skills do not get any worse as we age. In this chapter we find out about two writers. One of them wrote 19 novels. The other has written just one so far. One published her last novel at 91 and the other published her first at 93.

Margaret Ford –
The oldest person to publish her first novel

In 2019, Margaret Ford became the oldest person to publish her very first novel, called A *Daughter's Choice*. The book is the story of her early life.

Margaret was born in Blackburn in the North of England in 1926. Her father worked in her grandparents' pub. He was an alcoholic and was always gambling away the little money they had. When Margaret was 10, her father left the family. Margaret's mother had to look after Margaret and her older brother on her own. At 13, Margaret decided to leave school and get a job in a factory to help her mother. In the same year, World War II broke out.

Life during the war was difficult. Blackburn was bombed and a number of the boys Margaret knew died in the war. Margaret decided to live for the moment. She loved going to dance halls and the boys loved her. It was at a dance that she met Jim. Jim was an RAF pilot. They got married in 1946 and they travelled the world together.

The couple were married for 67 years. Not long after Jim died, Margaret started reading through the more than 630 letters he had sent to her when he was a soldier. It was while she was reading the letters that she had the idea to write the book. Three years later Margaret has a published book about her early life ... and is planning to write a second about her life with Jim.

P.D. James –
The Queen of Crime Fiction

Vocabulary

A *woman's* **maiden name** *is the surname or family name she had before she got married and took her husband's name.*

A **stage manager** *works in a theatre and is responsible for the practical arrangements for a play.*

A **civil servant** *is some one who works in a government department in a non-political role. The* **Home Office** *is the UK government department which is responsible for matters within the UK, including police and immigration rules.*

Phyllis Dorothy James was born in 1920 in Oxford. Like Margaret Ford, she left school at the age of 16 because her family was poor and because her father did not believe that girls needed a good education.

She worked in tax office for three years and then took a job as an assistant **stage manager** at a theatre in Cambridge. She married an army doctor during the Second World War and they had two daughters, born in 1942 and 1944.

Sadly, her husband returned from the war mentally ill and he spent the time until his death in 1964 in and out of institutions for mental illness. To support the family, James studied and started working in hospital administration. She also started to write fiction. Her first novel was published in 1962. It was a crime story about a police detective called Adam Dalgliesh. She wrote fourteen novels about Dalgliesh in her career. She published her novels under her **maiden name**, James.

After her husband died, she changed her job and started working as a **civil servant** in the **Home Office**. She continued working for the government until 1979 when she retired. She was made a Baroness in 1991 and so was a member of the House of Lords.

She wrote 19 novels and many more short stories. Her last novel was *Death comes to Pemberley*. It imagines how Jane Austen's story *Pride and Prejudice* might continue. It was published in 2011 when James was 91.

FLUID AND CRYSTALLIZED INTELLIGENCE

Vocabulary

Fluid can be a noun and means liquid (In hot weather you must drink enough **fluids**!) or an adjective. When it is an adjective, it means that something changes easily (The situation is **fluid**.) Here it means a kind of thinking which is flexible.

Crystals are beautiful rocks like amethysts. If something has **crystallised** then it means that it has become hard like a rock. Here **crystallised intelligence** means that the skills have become solid and reliable.

A **gadget** is a device or small machine that does something special. We sometimes talk about

electronic gadgets *and mean things like smart-watches, smartphones or tablet computers.*

Julie is ten years old. She is going to visit her grandparents for the weekend. While she is with them, Julie helps her grandfather with her new tablet computer and helps her grandmother set up WhatsApp on her smartphone.

Her grandfather helps Julie learn for her next test at school about the different countries in Europe and their capital cities. Her grandfather knows them all! Her grandmother helps Julie bake her mother's birthday cake and explains what to do. How does she know without looking at the recipe?

When they play games together, Julie always beats her grandparents at *Ligretto* where you have to quickly recognise the right cards but Julie is amazed at the questions her grandfather can answer when they watch *Who wants to be a Millionaire.*

The grandparents cannot believe how quickly Julie works out how to build her new Lego set although she does not even look at the instructions. She is so clever!

Julie is amazed at how her grandmother knows the names of *all* the flowers in the garden centre and how to look after them! She is so clever!

So, who is the more intelligent? Julie or her grandparents?

Fluid Intelligence

The psychologist Raymond Cattell explained that there are two types of intelligence. When we are young, our brain processes information quickly and we are good at keeping things in our memory. This means that we can quickly solve logical problems and learn new things. Our thinking is very flexible, or **fluid**. The kind of intelligence we have when we are younger is called **fluid intelligence**.

Crystallised Intelligence

As we get older, our working memory is not as good and we do not process information as quickly. This means we are slower at working out logical problems. But if we have done something similar before, then it is not a problem. We can use what we already know to solve new problems and learn new things. This intelligence is not as flexible and fluid but it is reliable. The knowledge has **crystallized**. Cattell called this **crystallized intelligence**.

Sometimes people think that they cannot learn when they get older, but this is not true. We just learn differently. We may not be as quick at learning how new **gadgets** work but we can build on the life experience we have and all the things we have learned in our lifetimes. This is why lifelong learning is so important. Learning means linking new knowledge to what we already know. The more you have learned in your lifetime, the more you can keep learning!

PARTNERS IN CRIME

Until now we have read about inspirational people who have done wonderful things. In this chapter, we are going to read about some people who are not so inspirational! In 2015 a group of pensioners were the topic of the news all over the world for stealing gold, jewellery and cash worth £14 million!

Vocabulary

This chapter has a lot of vocabulary about criminals and banks.

There are three different words for someone who takes something from someone else: **thief, robber** and **burglar**. **Thief** is a general word for anyone who steals something. They commit a **theft**. A **burglar** is someone who breaks into a building like a house or bank to steal something. The word for what they do is a **burglary**. A **robber** is someone who takes something and is often violent or threatens to hurt someone. They commit a **robbery**. When we talk about criminals, we often say they work together as a group and the word we use is **gang**. **Gang** can be used to mean a group of friends or workmen but the word is often used to have a negative meaning.

A bank often has a **vault**. This is a strongly protected room where money and other valuables are kept. They are often underground. In the vault, you find **safety deposit boxes** which is where each client's valuables are kept.

The men got underground by using the **lift shaft**. **Lift** is the British English word (BE). In the US they say **elevator** (AE). The men did not use the lift but the **shaft** which is the long vertical tunnel where the lift runs.

To catch the men, the police **bugged** their car. A **bug** is a small electronic device to listen to private conversations.

When criminals are caught and go to trial, they can decide whether they want to admit they did the crime or not. If they admit that they did the crime, we say they **plead guilty**.

There is one final word in the text which you might see with two different spellings: **jewellery** (BE) and jewelry (AE).

Hatton Garden is an area in central London. It is famous as a centre for the jewellery trade. There are 300 **jewellery** businesses in the area and 55 jewellery shops. Underground there is a maze of tunnels, offices and vaults.

On 2 April 2015, the staff locked up at the **safety deposit facility** in **Hatton Garden** in London and went home for the Easter weekend. When they returned after Easter, safety deposit boxes lay open and empty. Jewels and cash worth £14 million were gone and no-one knew who had stolen them.

A national newspaper had CCTV images which showed six older men breaking into the **vault**. The BBC called it the "largest **burglary** in English legal history". When they were caught, the British press called them 'Dad's Army' because all but one of the **thieves** were pensioners. *Dad's Army* is a very popular British comedy series from the 1970s about men too old to fight in the Second World War. The newspaper gave the men nicknames. They called them Mr Ginger, Mr Strong, Mr Montana, The Gent, The Tall Man and The Old Man.

So, who were these men, how did they do it and what happened to the gold and jewels?

On Thursday evening, Mr Ginger broke into the building. He then let the others in and two men climbed down the **lift shaft**. To get to the safety deposit boxes they had to get through a concrete wall which was 50 cm thick. They cut through this with a huge drill, making three holes which were big enough for a small person to fit through. Once they had drilled the holes, they had to use a ram to push the safety deposit boxes out of the way. After working for 11 hours, the ram broke and they had to give up.

The next night, some of the gang returned with a new ram and got into the vault. They emptied 73 safety deposit boxes, stealing jewels, gold and cash. In total, what they stole was worth £14 million.

How did the police find them?

On the second night one of the gang made a mistake. 74-year-old Kenny went to the vault in his own car, a rare and expensive Mercedes. The police followed Kenny when he met with the other gang members. They were not surprised to see who he met. All of the gang members were known to the police. The police **bugged** their cars and listened as the men talked about how they had done it and who was involved.

Three of the gang **pleaded guilty** before they went to trial. One of them, Danny (60 years old) told the police he had buried his stolen goods in a cemetery in London. He probably thought that it would look good if he gave back some of the goods. The police found a large amount of jewels and cash in one grave. A week later, Jones went to the cemetery with the police and showed them another grave with more stolen goods. He did not realise that the police had already found the first grave with a larger amount of the stolen goods.

Three more men were caught and put in prison. The final man, Mr Ginger or 'Basil' as the others called him, was free for three years after the robbery. He was the youngest of the group. He was only 55. When the police finally arrested him in March 2018, they found £143,000 worth of jewellery in his bedroom.

Of the £14 million stolen, less than £5 million has been recovered. The story is now famous. Two films and one TV series have been made about the elderly burglars.

DOES IT RING A BELL?

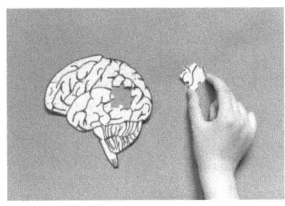

"I *saw what's-her-name today. You know ... our new neighbour ...*"
"*What did I go upstairs for? I can't remember!*"
"*Has anybody seen my keys?!*"

Does that sound familiar? Do you sometimes worry that you keep forgetting things? Is this normal? Is your memory failing?

First, we need to think about what we mean when we talk about the **memory**.

There are different types of memory. Scientists talk about a network which is made up of

- short-term memory
- working memory and
- long-term memory.

Short-term memory is the part of your memory you use when you remember a telephone number, a short shopping list or directions. You can keep about seven items in your short-term memory. However, you can remember more if you 'chunk' the information. This is the word that scientists use to mean putting a number of items together to form one new unit. You may remember a long telephone number, for example, by 'chunking' numbers together.

You usually try and keep things in your short-term memory by saying them to yourself over and over again, either out loud or in your head.

Your short-term memory does not change as you get older. You are still usually able to keep about seven things in your short-term memory. However, it is only short-term – you forget a telephone number really quickly once you have typed it into your phone! If you want to remember it for a longer time, you have to use the next part of the network.

Working memory is the part of your memory you use to *do* something with the information in your short-term memory. Imagine it is not a telephone number, but a different set of numbers. You are at the supermarket and have three things in your basket. You know you only have 10€ in your purse so you want to make sure you can pay for your shopping. You check the prices. Now you have four items in your short-term memory – the three prices of your shopping plus the 10€. You have to add the prices together and then take the total away from the 10€. The part of your brain that does this is the working memory.

Your working memory is also really important if you want to remember something for a longer time. How do we get something from the short-term or working memory into the long-term memory? Scientists say there are three steps to getting something into our long-term memory: **encoding**, **consolidation** and **retrieval**. We are going to look at each step.

Encoding

Let's imagine you meet your new neighbour and she tells you her name. She also tells you she comes from Paris and you notice she has a French accent. She tells you that her husband works for Renault, the French car company. She tells you they have three children and a dog. Two of the children run around her, chasing the dog as she is talking with you. In addition, she has blue hair and is wearing odd socks and you find this quite distracting. When you get home, you tell your partner that you have met the new neighbour. You can remember that she is French and has three children and a dog and has blue hair and socks that don't match ... but what's her name? You feel terrible. You should be able to remember her name! It is completely normal that you have 'forgotten' her name. You never knew it in the first place! You saw and heard all of the other information but her name was only briefly in your short-term memory. You never really noticed it. It was never put in the working memory to be '**encoded**'. Encoding is when we pay attention to something and work with the information in the working memory. We give it a meaning.

So how do you remember somebody's name? It helps if you use it when you speak to them. This at least keeps it is in the short-term memory for a little longer. You also need to give the information meaning and start to link it to something else which you already know. For example, if her name is Marie, you might remember that you had a friend called Marie at school. Or you might think of the famous scientist Marie Curie, or perhaps Queen Marie Antoinette.

Consolidation

The next step is **consolidation** which means that the information is 'stored' in the **long-term memory**. We do this by linking it to as many other things we know as possible. This is like putting the information in a big filing cabinet. The information about your new neighbour is in the same cabinet as the other neighbours and what you know about them and any other Marie's you know. The more old pieces of information the new memory is linked to, the easier it is to remember.

Retrieval

But a memory is only a memory if you **remember** it. This is the final and most important step called '**retrieval**'.

Your brain has lots of information. Every time you think of your new neighbour and try and remember her name, the pathway to the information is strengthened and it becomes easier and easier to remember it. This is how 'retrieval' works. The more often you have to remember it, the stronger the memory becomes in your long-term memory.

Memories are often linked to the place in which they are made. If you visited your old school, you would be reminded of the memories of your school days. That is also the reason that you cannot remember what you went upstairs to get until you are back downstairs in the living room! This is annoying but, on the other hand, it does give you a little bit more exercise which is also good for your brain!

And what if you are always looking for your keys? A 2013 study of young adults (18-34) and people over 55 in the US found that younger people are **twice** as likely to forget where they left their keys or forget to take their lunch to work or forget what day it is! So don't worry – it happens to us all! Anybody seen my house key?

MATURE STUDENTS

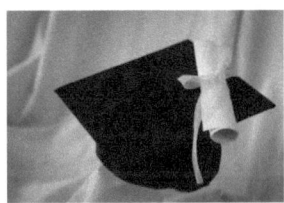

When you think of students, you probably think of young people. Sometimes people go to university after they have done something else. We call them mature students. In this chapter we will find out what made two mature students go to university and fulfil their dreams.

Giuseppe Paternò

Vocabulary

At a **brewery**, people brew or make beer.

A **surveyor** is someone who measures land. They either make maps or measure land for planning where buildings should go in a town or city.

If something is **well received** it means that people like it and often that lots of people praise it.

To **enrol** is another word for register or put your name down on a list. It is usually used for schools or universities.

To **graduate** means to successfully finish studying. To graduate, you often have to write a longer piece of work called a **dissertation**.

———

Guiseppe was born in 1924 in Palermo, Italy. He was the oldest of seven children and his family was poor. As a boy he helped his father with his job at a **brewery**. He loved learning and reading and saved his money to buy cheap books at the local market. His teachers called him a little wizard. However, his father decided he should leave school at the age of fourteen and start earning money.

During the Second World War, Giuseppe worked as a telegraph operator. Afterwards, he went to evening school and qualified as a **surveyor**. He now had a wife and a young family and needed to earn money to look after them so he took a job at the railway. All his life, he loved reading and learning, and was especially interested in philosophy.

He worked for the Italian railway for 42 years. When he retired, he decided to write a book about philosophy. It was **well received**. Giuseppe met a professor by chance. He asked the professor about starting a university degree and the professor did everything he could to help Giuseppe **enrol**.

At the age of 93, Giuseppe started his degree in history and philosophy at the university of Palermo. In the beginning he found it hard because he was not used to the technology the other students were using. He talked to his professor about giving up but the professor encouraged him to keep going.

Giuseppe was nearly finished with his studies when the Coronavirus started to spread in Italy in 2020. His son wanted him to do the final exams in the autumn but Giuseppe said he did not know whether he would live that long. He wrote his **dissertation** on a typewriter but in the end, he had to learn to use a computer to complete his courses.

Giuseppe **graduated** at the end of July 2020, just a few weeks before his 97th birthday. He says it was one of the happiest days of his life. He is now thinking of doing a Master's degree. His mother lived until she was 100, so he says he still has a few years.

He said his neighbours did not understand why he was studying when he was so old. They did not understand how important it was for him to fulfil his dream. His advice to older people is not to spend the rest of their lives staring at the television screen. It does not matter how old you are, you should never give up on your dreams.

Mary Hobson

Vocabulary

The qualifications at university are called degrees. The first degree is a Bachelor, the second is a Master's. If you study a science, then you have a BSc (Bachelor of Science) or an MSc (Master of Science). If you study a humanity, then you have a BA (Bachelor of Arts) or an MA (Master of Arts). When you study a humanity further, then you get a **PhD** *which means you are a Doctor of Philosophy. The doctor you go to when you are ill is an MD, a Doctor of Medicine.*

Have you ever thought of learning English so that you can read a novel by Charles Dickens in the original? Or maybe you would like to read *Don Quixote* in the original Spanish? Mary Hobson read a translation of Tolstoy's *War and Peace* while she was in hospital after an operation. She loved it but was sad that she could not read the original version. Then she decided that, actually, There was no reason that she could not and so she started learning Russian. She was 56.

At first, she wanted to go to evening classes but a friend offered to teach her, and eventually she understood enough to start reading *War and Peace*. It took her 2 years. Some years later, she phoned the University of London and asked whether they accepted older students. They said they did and Mary applied. At first it felt strange studying with students who were so much younger than her but she soon got used to it.

In 1991, she spent 10 months in Russia as part of her studies. It was a wonderful experience and she still visits the friends she made there at that time. 1991 also marked the end of the USSR and the Russian currency collapsed. Due to the fall in the exchange rate with the British Pound, she suddenly found she was rich! It was hard to buy food so she spent all her money on books. She bought over 200 books but then she did not know how to get them home. She finally had to ask school children to take three books each when they went on an exchange trip to the UK!

Mary really fell in love with Russian and decided to do a PhD which she finished when she was 74. She has translated a number of poetry collections by Pushkin and won awards for her translations.

In 2003, at the age of 77, she started to learn Ancient Greek and still continues to work on different projects. She believes learning kept her young as well as opening up a whole new interesting life.

LEARNING A LANGUAGE

Vocabulary

You might give someone a **head start** in a race by letting them start before you. You would probably only do this if you thought you could beat them anyway! If someone gets a **head start** in life, it means that they have an advantage over people who are otherwise in the same situation as them.

If you **pick something up**, it means that you learn it without any effort.

You may not notice something which is **subtle** because it is not so obvious.

*If you **cry over spilt milk**, you get upset about something bad which has happened which cannot be changed.*

Everyone knows that for learning languages, younger is better. Children start to learn a foreign language in primary school. Some children have their first lessons in kindergarten. Parents all around the world send their little ones to foreign language lessons early so that they can get a **head start**. It must be true. Why should we even try to learn a language when we get older? We will never succeed, will we?

This is what a lot of people believe. They believe that young brains learn better. However, it is not true! Research shows something very different. When we are talking about learning a language, we have to be very clear about *who* is learning it, *which* language you are talking about (the first or the second) and in *which context* they are learning it. We also need to understand that, when we learn a language, there are lots of things which play a part. It is not just about what happens in your head!

When you are born, you start learning your first language. Actually, you start before you are born! As babies grow, they learn their parents' language automatically. The more language they hear, the more easily they learn. Small children need a lot of input to learn a language. If the parents speak different languages to one another or a different language to the culture they live in, that is not a problem for the child. As long as they have enough input, then they can learn more than one language in this way. You do not sit a two-year-old down with a list of vocabulary and a grammar book! They just **pick it up** as they play with others and listen to people speaking. They learn it naturally.

To learn a language in this way, you have to be young. We can all think of people we have met who have moved to a new country and never really learned the language properly. Often if a family moves to a new country, young children will learn the language more quickly and more easily than their parents. There are probably lots of reasons for this. It is partly because their brains are more flexible (fluid intelligence) than their parents'. However, it is also because they get more input from people around them at school and because they can use their time to concentrate on learning the language. Their parents have other things to worry about, like finding work and somewhere to live, and it is more difficult for them to build relationships with people who speak the new language.

When you learn a language in a classroom, it is a different kind of learning to picking it up naturally. Firstly, you do not have as much input in the new language in the classroom. Children learning a new language at school have just one or two hours a week. That is not enough to learn the language in the same way they learned their first language(s). Researchers have found that when learning this way, *older children and adults learn more quickly*. This is probably because they learn by using their crystallised intelligence as well as their fluid intelligence. They have already learned *how to learn* and they can use this skill to learn the new language.

Should we send small children to language lessons for an hour a week? There are some advantages. Even though small children do not make the same progress as older children and adults, they are enthusiastic. If you can get a child interested in learning a new language when they are young, it can help their motivation when they are older. This is especially true if they become interested in the people who speak the other language and their country and cultures.

Although young children do not make the same progress as adults, there is one thing that is better learned when you are young. This is pronunciation. If children hear the language early, then their pronunciation will be better. It is more difficult for adults to sound like a native because they cannot hear **subtle** differences and have more difficulty repeating things correctly. Children are better at this ... if they have the right input.

Children need to *hear* the correct pronunciation to learn it. Teachers at kindergarten or primary school should speak the language well themselves so that they are good role models for the children.

If you are over the age of 10, it is unlikely that you will learn to speak a foreign language and sound like a native speaker. But there is no point **crying over spilt milk**! You cannot travel back in time and learn perfect pronunciation. But you can still learn a language and we will find out more about this in the final chapter of this book!

ACT YOUR AGE!

Our final biographies look at two famous actors: Christopher Lee and Anthony Hopkins.

Christopher Lee – From horror to fantasy

Vocabulary

The **Intelligence Service** is the government department which collects information about national and international enemies.

The **Armed Forces** is the word for a country's army, navy and air force. A **squadron** is a section especially of the air force.

A **baddie** is a character in a story who is evil or cruel. You can also use the word **villain**, but villain can be used for bad people in real life, too.

He played Dracula, Sherlock Holmes, an evil wizard and had roles in Star Wars and James Bond films. Then he recorded a number of heavy metal albums ... when he was over 90! If his life was made into a film, you would probably think it was unbelievable. His step-cousin was Ian Fleming who wrote the James Bond novels and he met many interesting people whom he would later play in films.

On 27th May 1922, Christopher Frank Carandini Lee was born in Belgravia, London. His mother was a Countess. He started performing in plays as a very young child at school.

In 1939, Lee finished school and joined the Finnish army fighting against the Soviet Union in the Winter War. He only spent two weeks in Finland and did not fight. In 1941, he joined the Royal Air Force (RAF). He was sent to South Africa and Rhodesia for training but he had a problem with his vision and was not allowed to fly any more. He joined the **Intelligence Service** and served in South Africa and Egypt. He nearly died when an airfield was bombed in Tunisia. He was moved to Malta where he had malaria six times within one year, but he survived. His **squadron** was sent to Italy and while he was in Naples, he climbed Vesuvius – it erupted just three days later. In the final months of the war in Italy, Lee was in a plane which crashed. Christopher Lee was only 23 years old but he had already escaped death several times!

After the war, Lee was sent to Austria and helped look for Nazi war criminals. He left the RAF in 1946 and went back to England. He could not decide what to do but his cousin suggested he should become an actor and Lee liked the idea. He went to acting school and had a number of very small roles.

His big breakthrough came when he started making films with the Hammer Film Productions, a British film company which made horror movies. He will always be remembered as Dracula and played the role 10 times. His first *Dracula* Film (1958) is said to be one of the best British films of all time.

Lee loved to play the '**baddie**' or **villain**. He played the baddie in the James Bond film *The Man with the Golden Gun* in 1974. He played the evil wizard Saruman in the films of *The Lord of the Rings* made by Peter Jackson in the early 2000s. Lee loved J.R.R. Tolkien's books and read them once every year and even met Tolkien. Finally, he played the evil Count Dooku in two of the *Star Wars* films.

However, he was not only an actor. He could also sing. He had a deep bass voice and recorded heavy metal albums. He released his last metal album at the age of 92.

This amazing actor kept working until the end of his life. He made his last film just three weeks before he died. During his career, he starred in 213 films but he will always be remembered as the frightening villain Dracula.

Anthony Hopkins – The oldest Oscar winner

Vocabulary

In some countries, young people have to spend a short period of time in one of the armed services. This is called **national service***.*

Philip Anthony Hopkins was born in 1937 in the small Welsh town of Port Talbot. His father was a baker. He was never very good at school. He preferred to draw or play the piano than do his school work. He studied drama in Cardiff and then did his **national service** in the British army for two years.

He began acting in the 1960s and won a number of awards for his work. He is well known for playing the murderer Hannibal Lecter in *The Silence of the Lambs* and won an Oscar for that role. He said that he had always been able to scare people. Even at school, he could tell a story in such a scary way that the girls always ran away screaming.

In 2019, Hopkins and Welsh actor Jonathan Pryce played *The Two Popes* in a film for Netflix. The film imagines Pope Benedict XVI and Pope Francis in the time just before Pope Benedict retired.

In April 2021, Hopkins became the oldest person to receive an Oscar, at the age of 83. He received it for his role in a film called *The Father*. The film tells the story of a man who is struggling with dementia. Hopkins himself keeps his memory active by learning poems and Shakespeare plays by heart. He said in an interview recently; "With age I have become wise and now I know that I know nothing." He normally lives in the USA and has both British and US citizenship. During the coronavirus pandemic, he returned to Wales and he said he makes the most of his time. He plays the piano, paints, reads and meditates.

As well as all his acting awards, Hopkins was knighted by the Queen in 1993.

Port Talbot

The town of Port Talbot is on the east of Swansea Bay, South Wales. It has just over 37,000 inhabitants. It has one of the biggest steelworks in the world which has been under the threat of closure for years.

In Wales, we say that there is something special in the water in Port Talbot. It is such a small town but so many great actors come from here. As well as Anthony Hopkins, Richard Burton was born here. Burton was one of the best paid actors of the 1960s and married Elizabeth Taylor … twice! Michael Sheen also comes from Port Talbot. He is best known for playing a vampire in the *Twilight* films and Tony Blair in *The Queen*, a film about the days following Princess Diana's death.

NEVER TOO OLD TO LEARN A LANGUAGE!

In this book, we have learned a lot about how our brains work and that getting older does not mean that we can no longer learn. We have also seen that older children and adults are more successful language learners in the classroom than younger children. But what about seniors? Why should seniors try and learn a language?

As we have seen, there is very little change in the brain as we grow older. Our thinking can get a little slower. Our memory is not quite so sharp as it used to be. However, we can still make new neurons and we can still learn. In fact, if we do learn something new, those new neurons will not die. We also learned that we have something that children and young people do not have:

crystallised intelligence. The older you get, the more you learn ... at least, the more you could learn! You can use all of your life experience to help you learn more and keeping mentally active is as important as keeping physically and socially active.

There are lots of reasons you may want to learn a language as you get older. Some people want to learn a language because they have friends or relatives who speak the language or live in a different part of the world. Other people have more time when they retire and want to travel more. They want to be able to order a coffee and buy a train ticket and talk to the people they meet. Some people want to continue using a language they spoke during their working lives and others because they are interested in the language and culture.

Is there another reason why it might be good to learn a language? Some researchers think that learning a language is especially good for your brain. Researchers found that people who spoke two or more languages showed symptoms of dementia about 4 ½ years later than people who only spoke one language. These studies looked mainly at people who had spoken at least two languages for most of their lives and they found that, even considering other things which help keep the brain healthy, speaking two or more languages was still a reason why dementia symptoms started later.

There are studies that even suggest that you do not need to be really "bilingual" to benefit from this effect. Some studies show that learning a language when you get older has a benefit for the brain. Why could this be?

Researchers think that learning a language makes your brain work really hard. Imagine you are in an English language class. People are talking in English; you read from your book, you have to think about the exercises and give answers, there is new vocabulary you have to try and remember, and so on. There is so much going on! Your brain has to try and make sense of all of that. You are giving your neurons something to do and creating lots of connections between them.

Let us look at learning vocabulary. Do you remember what we learned about how memories are made? First of all, we have to **encode** the information. We have to pay attention to it and notice it. When you read a new piece of vocabulary in a book, you have to notice it (*Oh! I don't know that word!*) and think about it (*I wonder what it means*) and then guess what it means from the words around it or look it up in a dictionary (*Oh! That's a useful word! I must remember that!*).

Then we have to **consolidate** the information. We have to link it to other things in our brains. Let us take a really difficult word from this book like **hippocampus**. You may know some ancient Greek and know that *hippo* means horse. Maybe you even know that *hippocampus* means 'seahorse' in Latin. Then you find out that this part of your brain looks a little like a seahorse and you can see a seahorse in your head! You remember seeing seahorses in the aquarium. You also remember that the hippocampus is really important for your memory. That is a good reason to remember it! All these connections start to consolidate or make the memory in your long-term memory.

Now comes the most important part: **retrieval**. Every time you think about the brain, you think about your hippocampus and how important it is and you see the seahorse. The more you think about it, the stronger the connection becomes.

When you learn a language, you have to do this again and again and all of this is really good for your brain. To benefit from this, you do not have to become like a native speaker! The important thing is that you challenge your brain to keep learning.

It is good to know that learning a language is doing you good but that is just one more reason to keep learning a language. For example, if you had not learned English, you could not have read this book!

So, think about all those new neurons! Give them a good chance of survival and learn a language!

For teachers

If you are a teacher and would like to use this book in your lessons, you can download some **free** lesson materials by going to my blog at

https://nevertoolatelanguage.wordpress.com/

or directly to the Payhip page:

https://payhip.com/SarahCurtius

Acknowledgements

A huge "thank you!" to my wonderful colleagues Annakiska, Lee, Mic and Michael for your input! Your corrections, queries and creative input are worth their weight in gold. Your suggestions made this book better. Any mistakes are still my own.

ABOUT THE AUTHOR

Sarah Curtius is an English teacher who lives near Hanover in Germany. She studied German and English in the UK and Germany and in 2019, she completed her MA in Applied Linguistics and TESOL (Teaching English to Speakers of Other Languages).

When she is not encouraging people to learn English, she loves to paint, sew and do any kind of handicraft. She is proud of her homeland of Wales which is the most beautiful place on earth!

ALSO BY SARAH CURTIUS

Coming later in 2021 ...

The 16th century writer Ben Johnson said that his friend William Shakespeare was "not for an age but for all time". People still love his stories and go to see traditional and modern performances of his plays. In this book you will find stories based on Shakespeare's plays and his characters, including the popular character of Bottom from *A Midsummer Night's Dream* and the young lovers from *The Merchant of Venice*.

CEFR B1/B2